The Inkweaver's Heartbeat

Romantic Poetry

Latsyrc Mironov

Copyright © 2025 Produced & Designed by
Latsyrc Mironov

Published by *Inkweaver Publishing Studios*
All rights reserved.

No part of this publication may be reproduced, stored in a retrieval system, or transmitted in any form or by any means—electronic, mechanical, photocopying, recording, or otherwise—without prior written permission from the author, except for brief quotations used in critical reviews, academic studies, or journalistic articles.

This book has been self-published with all reasonable efforts made by the author to ensure it is free of factual and typographical errors. The author assumes full responsibility and liability for the content herein, including but not limited to all views, representations, descriptions, statements, information, opinions, and references (collectively, the "Content").

ISBN: 979-8-218-68232-3

Standard Edition, 2025
Printed in the United States of America

For permissions or inquiries, contact:
Inkweaver Publishing Studios
inkweaverpublishingstudios@gmail.com

Golden Thread Collector's Edition
&
The Inkweaver's Heartbeat Tour
Visit
theinkweaversheartbeat.love

The Inkweaver's Contents
Golden Poems G*

Quintessent Kisses
I'm Writing You Something G*
Knots In Time
Breathing Soul G*
Scarlet Truth G*
Falling Embrace
Sunny Heart G*
Unbreakable Flame
Everything Noticed G*
Lover's Touch G*
Intimate Ecstasy
Say It Today
Particles Of Love G*
I'm Interested
Burning Tears G*
Never Learned
Wear Your Pretty G*
The Tootsie
Broken Pieces
Cosmic Child G*
My Soul & Me

Dedications

This is dedicated to the desire to be born for this—to the spiritual guidance and support of the unborn. It honors the threads of fate that pull us toward what is meant to be. A tribute to the devotion found in longing and union, to the ache that carves space for love, and to everything that sparks and inspires romantic connections to manifest and unfold.

It is both a celebration and a tribute to the sacredness and sacrifice of the feminine essence, from which all life emerges for the human experience. An offering to the unseen forces that shape our hearts and weave our destinies. To the poetry written in our Souls and the endless dance between longing and fulfillment.

Preface

The Inkweaver's Heartbeat invites you on an evocative journey through the elegant, raw, and deeply human dimensions of the Soul—woven together through poetic harmony.

This collection pulses with sensuality, intimacy, and passion, capturing love and longing in their purest forms. Through themes of desire, connection, and devotion, these poems offer a unique yet relatable reflection on life, striking a delicate balance between soulfulness and sensuality. This is poetry that speaks the language of the heart, evoking emotion beyond thought. It celebrates love's sensory landscapes, the sacredness of the heart, and the power of vulnerability and self-expression. For those who crave poetry beyond surface romance, this collection is an invitation into a deeper experience—where words are not just ink on this paper, but echos of your own Soul.

"Poetry from the heart is erotica of the Soul"
Latsyrc

Hello, Amore!

Find a quiet place. Take a deep breath. Center
yourself in your heart-space. Take your time, absorb
it as you read it slowly. Immerse yourself into
the emotions and feelings by bringing your complete
presence to this moment. I invite you to connect with and
experience the full extent of love that resonates with what
you read, reflecting the beauty that is in you.

It is my hope that experiencing the poems guides you to
new depths of self-understanding, self-love,
connection, healing, and a renewed perception
of the world around you.

The future is born through you. Your beating heart,
the core of the earth. Your womb, the path of the Soul.
Never forget that you are sacred and cherished by
men of light, the cosmic protectors of your
feminine essence.

So hold your shoulders firm Queen of earth.
Step up to the throne of your life, and Rule
your Kingdom amore!

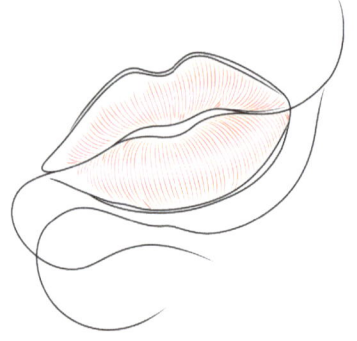

Quintessent Kisses

I kiss your Soul as if you are here,
No worry or fear, no distance to feel.

Kissing your essence, embracing its fullness,
Delighting in her light, truth, and purpose.

Kiss-drunk from the sweetness of your tenderness,
Adoring every part of your divine earthliness.
Kissing your heart in a passionate fire,
Indulging in her flames that fill all need and desire.

I kiss the dreams that dance in your sleep,
The quiet thoughts your heart hides to keep.
Each kiss a promise, a vow in the night,
To honor your Soul, your love, your light.

I kiss the tears that never fall,
The silent prayers, your spirit calls.
With lips that soothe, with care that mends,
Each kiss a love that knows no end.

With every kiss, I surrender to you.
With every kiss, I serve you.
With every kiss... I am one with you.

Birthday 3/23

I'm Writing You Something

I'm writing you something...
I'm sitting here, choosing the words,
As I watch the morning birds.

Trying to decide if the sentences
Should rhyme in twos or in thirds.
So far, it feels like it's going to mean more
With just my feelings, and less fancy words.

But I'm writing you something—
The thrill of not knowing everything it will reveal,
Yet it ignites my heart,
Knowing how it will make you feel.

The power it holds to move those pretty lips on
your face into a smile,
To make you blush,
As you try to hold it inside and not break out
crying.
Something to show how I'm your vase,
And you're the flowers.

I'm writing you something—it's something like
that.
Something to remind you again
Why your heart beats for me,
And she never beats flat.

So,
The only words deserving this ink
Are words of adoring you with how I think.
I'm writing you something to show you:
I love,
I care,
And I'm always, Here

Birthday 7/23

Ink Between Your Heartbeats

Knots In Time

They say time takes everything away—
The changing seasons, the blooms of May,
Faded memories, reasons to dance,
Moments lost to the endless expanse.

They say time is the sand that's falling in the hourglass,
A restless tide that sweeps from now to past.
It bends and breaks, leaves hearts to sigh,
A fleeting shadow beneath the sky.

But my time is not a clock, just a ticking thing;
It's a map of feeling, the space between everything,
A vessel of thought, both here and away,
Not bound by the edges of night or day.

They say time takes everything away,
But there are things to name; I know it doesn't—
Knots that bind the infinite whole,
The eternal truth of our heart and Soul.

The whispers you hear before you fall asleep,
And the treasures of our love your heart will keep.
These silent embers glow, though time may wane;
They live untouched by loss or pain.

They rise above time's binding strand,
To journey with us to a timeless land.
When bodies fade and Souls take flight,
These truths remain in endless light.

For what we share, is beyond distance and years,
Beyond the clockwork of mortal fears.
In the knots of this time, our dance of love is spun—
Infinite, eternal—and forever one.

Birthday 6/24

Ink Between Your Heartbeats

Breathing Soul

As long as it could breathe,
it still goes on; it never stops—
the urge, the need to show it's there.

It's always the same, as I wake or fall asleep,
just thinking, dreaming, endless ways
to show you how deeply you mean to me.

I love to lay and talk to you
as if you're with me.
Every thought I think, I speak,
as if you're right next to me.

For very long, I noticed this to be:
my heart just never changes course,
like the bow of a ship that knows its port,
where it needs to be—
a seasoned sailor, regardless to the mood of the sea.
As long as it could breathe.

I'll never get tired getting your attention.
Desires are endless descriptions
of everything I see in you and notice.
Forever reminding you, with all my affection,
without being shy or worrying discretion.

Because you're worth it—so worth it.
You're worth all there is in life to value.
Yes... it's been a long time.
As long as it could breathe.

Birthday 4/23

Ink Between Your Heartbeats

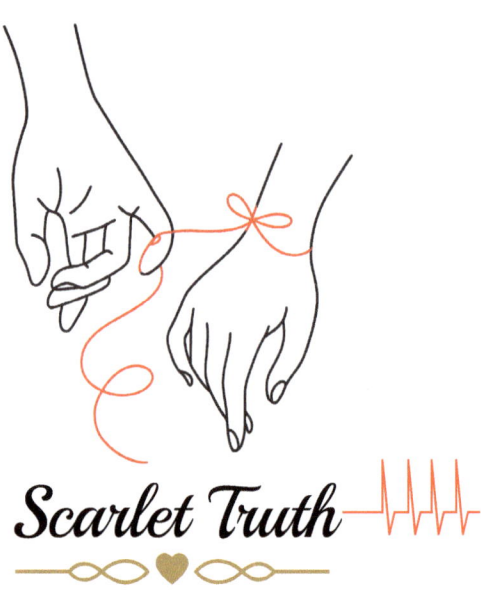

Scarlet Truth

A scarlet string is said to bind
Two destined Souls through space and time.
Across vast oceans, deserts wide,
Their hearts connect, though worlds divide.

Without yet meeting, they gently align,
A tether of love through the hands of time.
Soul to Soul, their truth appears,
Woman to man, in love's greatest frontier.

Some call it fable, mere chance, or lore—
A fleeting tale, nothing more.
But what they doubt, I hold as true,
For I feel the thread that ties me to you.

I feel you near, though miles apart,
I hear your voice inside my heart.
To me, it's always true—
This bond unbroken, forever anew.

Through all the storms and endless strife,
You are the rhythm, the pulse of my life.
Even when chaos would tear me apart,
You were the compass, the extra beat in my heart.

I know this truth will always remain:
Through every battle, joy, and pain,
That you're the one I'll find,
The one I'll hold—body and mind.

As long as I feel you, that's how I know—
The scarlet string will guide where to go.
Through time, through distance, through life's deep blue,
This string endures—forever true.

Birthday 11/24

Ink Between Your Heartbeats

Falling Embrace

I don't have it together every day.
There are days when I'm in pain, I'm hurt,
I'm irritated, or I'm worried.
There are those days I feel like I've failed.

The days I don't feel strong and frisky,
The days when my chest feels just heavy,
And it's harder to keep my focus steady—
Rehearsing the reasons, the ways to keep living.
I'm sorry... sometimes I have those days.

But it's days like those I remember what holds me.
I think of your hugs, your loving arms.
I think of what it's like to be caught by them,
Without fearing falling.

It's what helps me remember
That failure is never what's limiting,
And that your care is much more
Then just physically lifting.

So no matter how dark those days can get,
I always know when I'm in pain, suffering, and struggling—
I'm not afraid at all to fail.
Every way.
Every day.
Because falling, means I'll be in your arms.

Birthday 11/23

Ink Between Your Heartbeats

Sunny Heart

It's a sunny day in my heart,
A day to take you out to the park,
Feel the warmth with a peaceful walk.

It's a day to find you a wildflower,
A new way—to make you smile,
Another day to—dance with you for hours.

It's a day to look you in the eyes again—
To see my love reflecting light through them.

It's a sunny day...
I celebrate not feeling darkness from your heart.

A day to effortlessly push through all the difficult and hard,

Without feeling emotionally burdened—bruised or scarred.

When I say sunny—it doesn't mean it's not rainy or cloudy.
It means it doesn't matter what the weather is like,
Because of you, it's—always a sunny day in my heart.

Birthday 10/23

Ink Between Your Heartbeats

Unbreakable Flame

When life bends and breaks the fragile thread,
And dreams unravel, their colors fled,
Remember this truth—forgotten, divine:
Your heart is eternal, untouched by time.

The mind may waver, bound by strife,
Lost in the twisting, turning tides of your life.
Yet your Soul, unbroken, forever sings,
A melody deeper than the pain of earthly things.

Grief may shadow the brightest day,
But your essence glows; it cannot decay.
This pain, though heavy, is not your whole;
It does not define the depths of your radiant Soul.

So for the wounds to heal and your tears to dry out,
Please, don't let your mind close your precious heart.

Birthday 1/25

Ink Between Your Heartbeats

Everything Noticed

I do this thing before I go to bed,
I count the moments, the words unsaid.
Every detail, no matter how small,
Everything noticed in you, I try to recall.

The shadows your lashes cast on my chest,
Where time slows down and moments last.
A language unspoken, soft as the rain,
That tells me a story that words can't contain.

I fight my mind to capture it tight,
Each fleeting detail, like a beam of light
Everything noticed, each beat of your heart,
A rhythm that sets all beauty apart.

Everything noticed, the brush of your hand
The way you move, like waves on the sand.
Not even silence can steal what I see,
For every trace of you, lives within me

The way your presence colors the room,
A fleeting sunrise dissolving gloom.
Every glance and every sigh,
Are like a thousand verses passing by.

In my quiet gaze, all truths align,
No part of you, escapes this heart of mine.
For in this love, nothing is lost,
Every moment is cherished, no matter the cost.

Birthday 10/24

Ink Between Your Heartbeats

Lover's Touch

I touch you when you don't even notice,
When you're just going about your day.
I touch you silently, even without having words to verbally say.

I don't just touch you to lift your beauty, your happiness, your bliss.
I touch what bothers you, hurts you, brings you pain.
I touch the grief, the sorrow—
Because I know how to touch it...
In a way that can... take it away.

I love to do this. It's why I live.
My favorite—when I brush my hand on your cheeks
As you're asleep in my arms,
To show you I'm there with you in your dreams.

It's with my emotions, my look at you, my smile,
my sweetness—gentleness, our memories.
It's with every part of me I share with you,
Without withholding or sparing.

No, I don't just touch you the way skin feels
When pressed—It's the way the heart feels when it
knows it's finally...
Intimately... addressed.

Birthday 3/23

Ink Between Your Heartbeats

Intimate Ecstasy

I love to feel you close to me,
A touch that sets my spirit free.
Our breath aligns, the heart beats new,
As every moment draws me to you.

I love the visions that you share,
The way you see me, raw and rare.
You shine your light where shadows hide,
Unraveling all I hold inside.

I love the shivers, soft yet strong,
The way you've held me all along.
A rush that lingers, pure and deep,
A burn that wakes me from my sleep.

The heat and warmth, flooding its course,
The pulsing of my heart, rhyming with yours.
You move through me like liquid fire,
Igniting depths of pure desire.

With every touch, my world is yours,
A love unchained that Soul adores.
Like waves that kiss the endless shore,
I'm yours today and evermore.

No longer two, but one we stand,
Bound in heart, not just by hand.
Under the moon, in tangled sheets,
Our form takes charge, and life repeats.

Birthday 3/23

Ink Between Your Heartbeats

Say It Today

There are things in life we long to share,
Words that linger, suspended in the air.
Those moments when time feels thin,
When the need to speak begins within.

It happens in silence, while walking alone,
Sometimes the thoughts as I'm driving home.
Even in rain, I'm searching for a way
To capture the things
I can't forget to tell you today.

I don't want to wait for a better chance,
To leave these words to happenstance.
What matters most can't be delayed,
For life moves quick, and moments don't last.

I cannot hold what heart burns to give,
The words that prove how deeply I live.
For love, for you, they must find a way,
To come to life and not, just fade away

As time is tender, and it slips so fast-
What remains unspoken may, forever last.
So hear me now, as I stop the world for this,
Let my heart, my voice, fulfill this will of mine

Birthday 9/24

Ink Between Your Heartbeats

Particles Of Love

My love unfolds like a rose in the night,
A fire that dances in soft golden light.
Particles of love flow deep to your core,
Ignited by me, your spirit is whole.

Love holds many things within its embrace,
Many forms, many shapes, many shades to trace.
But do you wonder—how would it appear,
If love was a tangible essence in front of us here?

Through actions, emotions, and looks in disguise,
A secret language hidden from the eyes.
From thoughts to touch, from heart to art,
Two separate things, yet never apart.

How we see each other, a mirror divine,
Revealing truths where the stars align.
How we are loyal, how we evolve,
In this mystery of love, we come to dissolve.

These particles exist beyond confinements of space,
Bound together by a quantum lace
Me and you—a magnetic force
Spinning in sync, on love's endless course

These particles, timeless and free,
Reside in a love that eternity sees.
Me and you, a boundless connection,
Our eternal form, in nature's reflection.

Birthday 12/23

Ink Between Your Heartbeats

I'm Interested

I'm not interested in just your body's beauty,
love—
I'm interested to see how you use your makeup
and how you get ready for your day.
I'm interested to see you dance, create beauty with
your mind and your precious hands.

I'm interested to see you soulful, watch you
play with things you find so fun and joyful.
I'm interested to hear your thoughts
on what one should do to remain hopeful.

I'm interested in how you think—
what you find odd, what you find extravagant,
enlightening, elegant, exciting.
I'm... so interested in that,
because they're the most attractive things I see,
from all the uniqueness I know you to be.
I'm interested.

I'm interested to hear you speak
on what you think the world needs—
and all about the news, the forecasts
of your favorite Instagram feeds.
I'm interested to hear all about your crazy day,

everything that happened, exactly as it did
today—
like how you struggled to contain
how your makeup melted in the rain.
I'm interested.

I'm interested to see you blush,
as you accidentally show your kinks and quirks,
just for you to watch me accept them,
see them as nothing more than life's art-filled
perks.

I'm interested to be here—
hear you, hold you, guide you, heal you.
I'm so interested in that,
knowing that you'll always need me, see me,
and remember how to feel me.
Yes, love, I'm interested.

And I'll be interested,
no matter how much age your body holds
or how many wrinkles, curves it forms.
I'll love you the same way, as I see you every day—
yes, interested in you.
Always.

Birthday 3/23

Ink Between Your Heartbeats

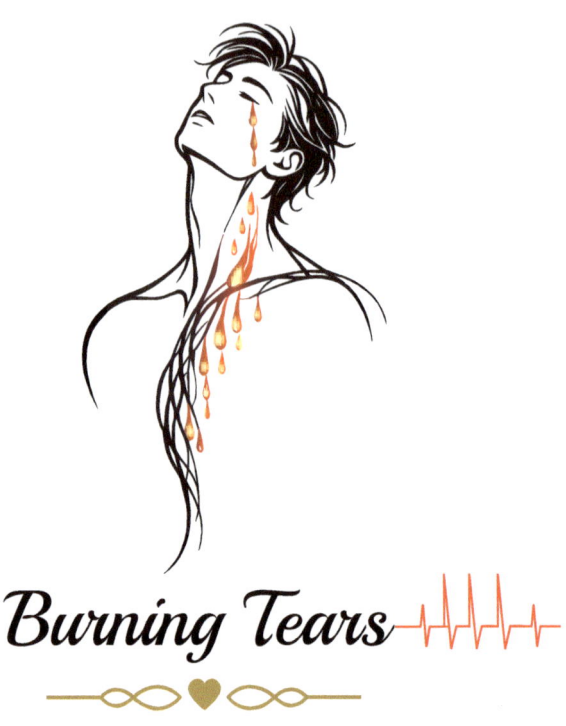

Burning Tears

I cry when I touch your body.
It's not because I'm lonely, depressed, or sad—
No, there's no grief when I cry like that.

It's the tears in joy of never-ending
emotions, memories, from many days pending,
all the days, spent patiently waiting for you.

I cry when I touch your body
because your beauty burns, like fire touching wool.
There is nothing like it—it's so heavenly, magical, and pure.

I cry when I touch your body
because it fills my mind, with what it carries,
all that longs, through it to be born.
Every touch... it shows me the future,
where we are happy and never without each other,
alone.

I cry when I touch your body
because it's the most peace and comfort I can ever
come to know—

when my heart can fully soak in everything, it can
sense of you, and behold.

I cry because... I never want it to be the last time.

Birthday 11/23

G*

Ink Between Your Heartbeats

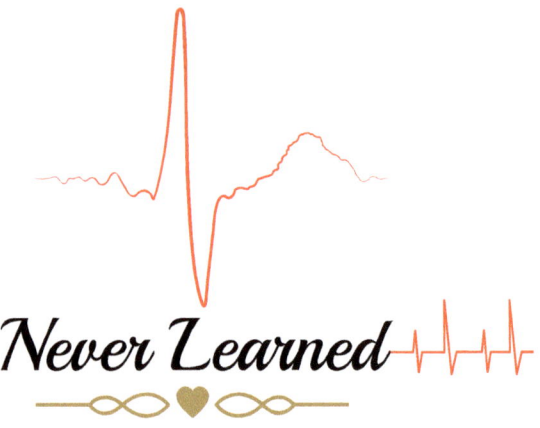

Never Learned

Growing up, so many things I tried so hard to learn.
Some of them were pointless—just something new for me to try to do.

Some of them were fun, exciting,
but never so to charge my heart like lightning.
I struggled to find the feeling,
believing others, that the good things
need to be learned to have meaning.

They told me love is earned with time,
built through lessons, reasons, signs.
But I know, that all my trials, all my plans,
will fade away, when I touch your hands.

I never have to learn to see
the way your Soul speaks endlessly to me.
I never have to train my heart
to love you whole, in every part.

I never have to search to find
the beauty woven by your mind.
Like stars that shine without a cue,
my body knows—what beats for you.

I never have to practice care,
to bring you comfort, when life seems unfair.
I never have to learn your needs—
for they already echo in my heart with ease

Nothing taught me how to see
that you were always meant for me.
Not a single lesson made me wise—
As it's already written, deep within my eyes.

And now I know—it's clear and true—
I was never meant to learn of you.
There are no lessons, no failed tries—
just born to love you, with all of my life.

Birthday 8/23

Ink Between Your Heartbeats

Wear Your Pretty

I want you to do something for me.
I want you to look at yourself
until you notice everything that is pretty.

You can't see this kind of pretty with a mirror.
It's the kind that's beyond sight, touch—
it's only inner.

It's the kind of pretty that is called, recognize.
They're not things that fade or smear, called beauty.
They don't change with age; they don't have a birthday.

It's the things that make you vulnerable and shy,
your sacrificing efforts, everything that makes you cry.
It's all the days you suffered and shrugged,
and how you still know, you deserve to be loved.

That... is your pretty.

So let today be a day,
you notice a different pretty.
Even if your life can seem a mess though,
and you don't feel successful,
please, still wear your pretty.

Wear her beautifully and proud.
Wear it through your face—
not just what you put on it.

However you wear it,
just never forget—you are it.
Not the things that make you look, temporarily pretty,
but how you recognize the things within you
that are your real pretty.

Birthday 10/23

Ink Between Your Heartbeats

The Tootsie

There is this lady— that haunts my dreams,
A moving force as she appears
She has no crown, no royal throne
Yet reigns within my heart alone.

Her eyes are stars in velvet skies,
A spark of love that never dies.
Deep as ocean, warm as fire,
They pull me close in wild desire.

She wears a smile, so bright and neat,
A spell so charming, my Soul's defeat.
Her hair cascades around her neck,
Like liquid light in moonlight's sight.

Her touch is soft, her voice asleep,
A hush where love and longing meet.
each word a promise, each sigh complete,
She stirs my Soul with silent heat

Her lips, a poem I long to read,
Words that touch, and plant a seed
Her body flows, both fierce and fine,
Like art alive, in flesh divine.

And when we meet, the stars will stand,
Two hearts aligned, by fate's own hand.
A simple glance, a fleeting chance
Yet love will weave it in our dance

And when she knows, when heart ignites,
I'll pull her close in silver light.
She'll trace her longing, in a gentle press,
And in my arms, she'll whisper, yes.

Birthday 3/23

Ink Between Your Heartbeats

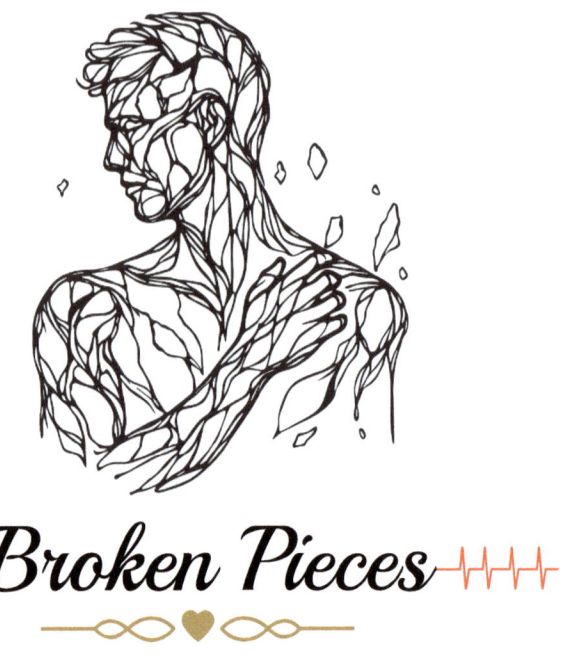

Broken Pieces

What do you see when you look at me?
Do you see a man, as if he's sculpted from a single piece of marble,
or do you notice, all the shattered pieces?
Because—that is what I am

If you're expecting wholeness that doesn't come from broken pieces,
you won't find it here.

If you're expecting joy without the days of pain and tears,
I don't have that either.

If you're expecting things that appear nicer than
they really are—
you must call beauty something different.

Because my beauty is all the broken parts that
made me who I am,
none of which are even close to the word
perfection.

But if you desire that which lasts longer than a
lifetime,
that is what I have...

My love for you—it comes from all those broken
pieces.
The pieces that look whole... to only you.

Birthday 12/23

Ink Between Your Heartbeats

Cosmic Child

My journey starts before the eyes saw clouds,
Before skin felt its first pressure of touch.
My journey starts before the stars were set in place,
before light and shadow began their chase.

Before the sky could cradle the sun,
before the rivers had learned to run,
before the wind had found its voice,
I drifted free—and without choice.

No weight, no name, no fate to claim,
no form to bind, no need to tame.
A breath of love, a spark untied,
a Soul unchained, a Cosmic Child.

Yet I wondered—what is it like?
To see the dawn and chase the night,
to taste the rain, the ocean's mist,
to know the warmth of a first kiss.

To dance where mortal spirits tread,
where dreams take root and hope is fed
To wake and breathe, to laugh, to cry,
to touch the earth, yet kiss the sky

So here I stand, yet not confined,
a traveler both in flesh and mind.
A ripple formed in endless space,
Like a shadow dancing out of place

An eternal Cosmic Child, I am.
A leaf from one vine, a pulse beyond time
I was never born.
I never die.
Yet—I always AM.

Birthday 10/24

Ink Between Your Heartbeats

My Soul & Me

I've always wondered why he was chosen.
For many years, I questioned why.
I watched him grow,
felt every moment of his joy and pain.

He's a weird fella, even though he's called
baby-cute.
The average things in life are not important
if they're not loving, soft, and mellow.

He's the type for deep, abnormal conversation
over boujee wine or tea.
He's the type to tell you he feels
the changes in the atmosphere,
without needing to get high.

He has a knack for writing things
that take his breath away—

To him, the spaces between inhales feel sweeter,
as if they show him
there's more to life than just struggling to breathe deeper.

He's the kind of romantic
you don't meet for love at the bar—
the kind that's born with poetry deep inside his heart,
saved in Soul before his life,
ready for the perfect moment... way ahead of time.

Only now do I know
why you chose this life to be him,
and how you knew that he could make it.
It's through that love within—
he doesn't need to live a single day to fake it.

Yes, that Soul is me.

Birthday 10/23

Ink Between Your Heartbeats

The Inkweaver's Aphorisms

A woman will love with all her being—but she stays when she is loved with all of your presence.

He is the right man if the only time he ignores you is when he's daydreaming your poetry.

Make it a habit to read each other something romantic before bed, even if it's just a poem from this book.

If she is deep, fluent in energy, has moonlight in her eyes, and gets butterflies from words she reads, her weakness isn't diamonds—it's muscles and poetry.

A woman will remember the way you made her feel long after she forgets what you said or did.

Stop with just the flowers. Take a pen, close your eyes, and write from the center of her

being within you. The essence of just a sentence,
etches reality with its summoned
presence and outlives a bouquet of flowers by a
stretch of infinity.
Still buy her flowers.

A tear deserves a thousand smooches. Love is
never too much, and affection is never
excessive. If someone tells you otherwise, run—the
love of a thousand smooches is
elsewhere.

A developed man isn't afraid of a woman's
strength. He is captivated by the beauty of
how she carries it.

Love isn't about being identical; it's about
complementing—like sunlight and shadow
painting the same masterpiece.

A man who knows how to love you will kiss your
scars as he does the most beautiful
parts of your heart.

Her Cramps Cure: Detox tea. Clean the house. A
massage. Heating pad. Chocolate.
Forehead kisses. Early bedtime. Read her a poem
from this book.

The Poetry Of Two Couples Bonding Activities

- Annual Poetry Reflection: Pick a poem and write a short note about why you chose it and how it resonates with your relationship—romantically, mentally, and emotionally... Store these in an envelope and read them together in the future, like for special occasions. See how your love story unfolds through poetry over time.

- The Doghouse Redemption: Whenever one of you is in the doghouse, they must read a golden poem to the other. The goal? To create the most awkwardly romantic moment in history—one so cringeworthy that it dissolves tension and leads straight into a heartfelt (and possibly tea-fueled) reconciliation.

- Bathtub Poetry Ritual: Spray the book with waterproof spray (or get creative with laminated printouts).
Run a warm bath, light candles, and play soft, peaceful music. Read to each other until the water

turns cold—because nothing says romance like pruney fingers and poetic whispers.

• Midnight Poetry Confessions: Keep the book on your nightstand. Whenever one of you wakes up in the middle of the night, read a random poem to the other in a sleepy, half-dreamy state. Romantic?
Absolutely. Confusing? Maybe. Memorable? Always.

• Pick a poem from the book and rewrite it as a love letter to each other. Bonus challenge: Try writing it in the style of a Shakespearean sonnet, a cheesy rom-com script, or a dramatic breakup-and-reunion scene.

• Hide the book somewhere in your home, find something in one of the poems to use as a clue; handwrite the clue from one of the poems into a message, hinting your partner to it. The reward? A cozy reading session together once they find it.

• Take turns picking a poem from the book and dramatically performing it while the other judges your delivery. Categories can include "Most Passionate Performance," "Most Unintentionally

Hilarious," and "Best Use of Dramatic Hand Gestures."

- Randomly flip to a poem and let it set the tone for your next date night. If it's about passion, go dancing.
If it's about longing, write each other love notes. If it's about heartbreak... well, maybe just get dessert and laugh about it.

- One of you has to read a poem to the other in song form—but you can only use melodies from famous pop songs. Imagine a love poem sung to the tune of "Bohemian Rhapsody." Legendary.

- Sit nose-to-nose and take turns whispering lines from a poem to each other. Whoever blushes, giggles, or melts into a puddle of romance first loses.

- Read a poem to each other, but with a hilarious twist—one of you must read it as if you're a suspicious, grumpy oldie that doesn't believe in true love.

Romantic Gifting Collector's Edition
The Inkweaver's Golden Thread

" There is suspense in her pulse, a half breath apart
A golden gasp, the prelude of heart.
Love holds it's breathe, as Soul plays her part "

🧡 Enveloped Customizable Letter
Printed on Custom Paper
🧡 Custom packaging
🧡 Extended Collection Of Golden Poems
🧡 More Couples Games & Inkweaver Aphorisms
🧡 Secret Custom Book Decorations
🧡 Author's Golden Ink Signature
🧡 Golden Thread Edition Golden Seal
And More...

The Perfect Gift

Mothers Day, Father's Day, Valentine's Day,
Birthdays, Anniversaries, Baby Showers,
Weddings, Reunions, etc. . . light up their life
with The Inkweaver's Heartbeat Golden Thread

Available at The Inkweaver's Heartbeat

Website

Thank you for being a part of this journey. *May my poetry always find you in* ***love****—with him, with her, with your dog, with your mini-pig, with* ***all of life****, and most importantly, with* ***YOU****.*

www.ingramcontent.com/pod-product-compliance
Lightning Source LLC
Chambersburg PA
CBHW042309150426
43198CB00001B/21